When *Prayer* Doesn't Work:

Identifying And Overcoming Barriers

COPYRIGHT © [2024]
All rights reserved

No part of this publication may be reproduced, distributed, or transmitted in any form or by any means, including photocopying, recording, or other electronic or mechanical methods, without the prior written permission of the copyright owner, except in the case of brief quotations embodied in critical reviews and certain other noncommercial uses permitted by copyright law.

ISBN: 978-1-958052-28-0

DEDICATION

I dedicate this work to all who struggle with prayer in the midst of frustration, grief, anger, hurt, and doubt. Faith is undoubtedly a journey—a path where some find their faith deepening, while others may feel distant or even disconnect from it altogether. My deepest hope is that this book speaks to people at all stages of faith, whether you are a beginner or well-seasoned in your spiritual walk.

Though written from a Christ-centered perspective, I believe this work can offer insights and encouragement to individuals from all faith traditions. May this work be a blessing to you.

TABLE OF CONTENTS

Dedication iii

Introduction. vii

CHAPTER 1: Old Ways 1

CHAPTER 2: Following Instruction 7

CHAPTER 3: Looking Beyond 13

CHAPTER 4: His Will, His Timing 17

CHAPTER 5: Out of your comfort zone 21

CHAPTER 6: Believing. 25

CHAPTER 7: Death, Dying, Healing 31

CHAPTER 8: Relationships in Marriage 37

CHAPTER 9: The Importance of Preparation in Prayer. . . . 43

CHAPTER 10: Praying Through Anger and
              Disappointment 47

CHAPTER 11: Final Words. 51

INTRODUCTION

Have you ever prayed so fervently for something—poured your heart out in prayer, fasted devoutly, consecrated yourself continually—yet your prayers seemed to go unanswered? In this book, I aim to explore this feeling of spiritual frustration through the lens of the 7th chapter of the Book of Joshua, focusing specifically on five key areas of prayer: marriage, death, sickness, tragedy, and anger.

What is Prayer?

Prayer is more than simple communication with God. It is deeper than just presenting a list of wants and needs. Prayer is an intimate moment with God—a sacred time when we open our hearts and souls to Him. While prayer can be a communal experience, like when we gather in church as the Bible instructs, *"Forsake not the assembling of yourselves together"* (Hebrews 10:25), it is also a deeply personal act. Throughout the Bible, we see numerous examples of men and women who prayed both individually and collectively.

Personal prayer, done in solitude, is just as important as corporate prayer. God longs to hear our innermost thoughts, our joys, and our struggles. Not every blessing or burden needs to be shared with the world, or even with those closest to us, like our spouse, best friend, or confidant. Some things are meant to be between us and God.

Why Does Prayer Sometimes Feel Ineffective?

As a pastor, I've had countless conversations with people who grapple with life's complexities—struggles in their faith, their marriages, and their various relationships. In my role as a mental health professional, I have also worked with couples trying to navigate their way through challenges. This book is designed to help those who feel like their prayers aren't working. Through sharing personal stories, I'll offer thought-provoking questions to help readers explore their emotions, all while offering a new perspective that may aid them during their time of despair or in their faith journey.

The Premise

The inspiration for this book came during a trip to Tennessee. I was there to support my cousin, a fellow pastor and author, at his book launch. On Friday, the night before the event, we prepped materials, products, and merchandise. Saturday was the big day, full of setup and managing the event. My task was to create a self-care experience room based on my book, *Self-Care: Let's Start the Conversation*. After a long day of running the experience room and breaking down the setup afterward, we were all completely exhausted.

As we traveled back to my cousin's house, there were audible sighs of relief after a full day's work. My cousin, utterly worn out, looked at me and said, "Cousin, it would be a blessing if you could preach at one of the services tomorrow." Without hesitation, I replied, "Whatever you need, cousin."

That night, I went to bed early so I could wake up refreshed and ready to study. The next morning, as I prayed, the Lord directed my attention to Joshua, Chapters 5-7. This passage became the foundation for the message I preached—and now, it serves as the inspiration for this book.

I pray that the themes and lessons of this book will help you, the reader, gain a deeper understanding of prayer, especially in the most difficult moments of life. Whether you are struggling with unanswered prayers or searching for a renewed connection with God, my hope is that this work will provide comfort, guidance, and a new perspective on your faith journey.

CHAPTER 1

OLD WAYS

If you are new to scripture, this story begins with the biblical character Joshua. After Moses led the children of Israel out from the bondage of slavery under the Egyptian Pharaoh, they spent more than 40 years in the wilderness. During this time, God was preparing a place for them: the land of Canaan, also known as the Promised Land or the Land of Milk and Honey. However, before they could enter, the children of Israel often became unruly and disobedient. They frequently complained and questioned both God and Moses' leadership.

Moses, the leader at the time, became so frustrated with their behavior that he disobeyed a direct instruction from God. As a result, God told Moses that because of his disobedience, he would not be allowed to enter the Promised Land (Numbers 20). After Moses' death, God passed the mantle of leadership to Joshua, a faithful servant and fierce warrior who had served under Moses.

Joshua was called by God to lead the children of Israel out of the wilderness and into the Promised Land, but the task was far from easy. Not only did Joshua have to contend with the people's doubts and fears, but he also had to lead them in various battles along the way.

Feeling a personal connection to this story, I was led by the Spirit to focus on chapters 5 and 6 of the Book of Joshua. These chapters recount Israel's miraculous victory over Jericho, achieved through prayer and unconventional battle strategies—reminding us that God's ways are not always what we expect, but they are always perfect.

This story of Joshua teaches us profound lessons on obedience, faith, and the power of trusting God's plan, even when we don't fully understand it. Through Joshua's unwavering trust in God, we see that victories are not won by human strength but by following divine direction.

Joshua 6:1-5 (ESV)

The Fall of Jericho

6 Now Jericho was shut up inside and outside because of the people of Israel. None went out, and none came in. 2 And the Lord said to Joshua, "See, I have given Jericho into your hand, with its king and mighty men of valor. 3 You shall march around the city, all the men of war going around the city once. Thus shall you do for six days. 4 Seven priests shall bear seven trumpets of rams' horns before the ark. On the seventh day you shall march

around the city seven times, and the priests shall blow the trumpets. 5 And when they make a long blast with the ram's horn, when you hear the sound of the trumpet, then all the people shall shout with a great shout, and the wall of the city will fall down flat, and the people shall go up, everyone straight before him."

Before the battle of Jericho, Joshua was known as a fighter—a mighty man of valor who was accustomed to leading battles from the frontlines. Throughout his military career, he displayed strength and courage, relying on his combat skills to lead Israel to victory. However, as the leader of Israel in this pivotal moment, we see a shift in his role. When God gave him specific instructions for conquering Jericho, the strategy was unlike anything Joshua had ever known. God's commands did not rely on the use of military might or Joshua's strength as a warrior.

This time, the victory would come through obedience and faith, not force. God provided the who, what, when, where, and how—clear and detailed instructions. Joshua was no longer called to be the one at the forefront of the battle but the one who was called to listen. His primary task was to lead the people in following God's plan, even though the method was unconventional.

The significance of this story lies not only in the miraculous fall of Jericho but also in the shift it symbolizes in Joshua's leadership. It highlights a moment when Joshua had to rely fully on God's voice rather than his own abilities. The plan was precise: march around the city for six days, and on the seventh day, circle it seven times, blow the trumpets, and shout. It was a test of faith and patience, not strength.

This scenario teaches us a valuable lesson—sometimes, our greatest victories come not from our natural strengths or what we're accustomed to, but from obedience and trust in God's direction. When we follow His plans, even when they don't make sense to us, we allow God to demonstrate His power in ways that go beyond human understanding. Joshua's willingness to listen, rather than act out of his usual place of strength, was key to Israel's victory. This shift from fighting to listening is a powerful reminder that true success often comes from surrendering our ways and trusting God's plan.

Reflection

Let's take a moment to reflect. What if Joshua had continued in his usual way of handling things, relying on his strength and battle experience rather than God's guidance? The outcome would likely have been very different. Are you, perhaps, approaching your current season of life using methods that are no longer productive? As we mature and enter new stages of life, with added responsibilities and challenges, it's essential to seek God's direction on how to navigate them. Are you stuck in old patterns of thinking or acting—ways that might actually hinder the progress, answers, and clarity you're seeking?

Sometimes, we can be so focused on *doing* that we forget to *listen*. We may rush ahead, relying on familiar strategies, instead of being still and allowing God to guide us in new ways. But what if God is calling you to pause, reflect, and listen to His voice rather than continuing in your own strength?

Things to Consider

- Where am I in my life right now?
- What habits, thoughts, or strategies do I need to let go of?
- In which areas of my life do I need to be still and patient?

Making the Prayer Personal

Dear Lord, this is_____coming before You today. I realize that I am in a new season of life, and I need your wisdom to help me let go of _____, _____, and _____. Lord, guide me to understand what this stage of my life requires and give me the clarity to see your way more clearly. Help me refrain from using old thoughts and mentalities, especially as I encounter repeated or new challenges on this faith journey. I trust in your perfect guidance and timing. Amen.

Scripture for Meditation

Proverbs 3:5-6

Trust in the Lord with all your heart, and do not lean on your own understanding. In all your ways acknowledge Him, and He will make straight your paths.

CHAPTER 2

FOLLOWING INSTRUCTION

After reading Joshua chapter 6, it becomes clear that Joshua's obedience to the Lord's instructions led to victory in the battle of Jericho. Part of God's directive to Joshua is detailed in verses 18-19:

18 "But you, keep yourselves from the things devoted to destruction, lest when you have devoted them you take any of the devoted things and make the camp of Israel a thing for destruction and bring trouble upon it. **19** But all silver and gold, and every vessel of bronze and iron, are holy to the Lord; they shall go into the treasury of the Lord."

As the Israelites continued their journey to the Promised Land with God's guidance, things did not go as expected in the next battle. Upon reading Joshua chapter 7, it becomes evident that despite the clear instructions from God, one of the Israelites disobeyed by taking an accursed thing, hiding it in their tent.

This disobedience resulted in the loss of lives and Israel's defeat in the battle of Ai (Joshua 7:1).

2 "Joshua sent men from Jericho to Ai, which is near Beth-aven, east of Bethel, and said to them, 'Go up and spy out the land.' And the men went up and spied out Ai. **3** And they returned to Joshua and said to him, 'Do not have all the people go up, but let about two or three thousand men go up and attack Ai. Do not make the whole people toil up there, for they are few.' **4** So about three thousand men went up there from the people. And they fled before the men of Ai, **5** and the men of Ai killed about thirty-six of their men and chased them before the gate as far as Shebarim and struck them down at the descent. And the hearts of the people melted and became as water."

As I continued reading the chapter, a passage that stood out to me begins in verse 6:

6 "Then Joshua tore his clothes and fell to the earth on his face before the ark of the Lord until the evening, he and the elders of Israel. And they put dust on their heads."

At first glance, in the aftermath of tragedy, this seems like a natural response—turning to God in prayer. In fact, as Christians, this is what we are taught to do. Joshua, in his grief, engages God in conversation:

7 "And Joshua said, 'Alas, O Lord God, why have you brought this people over the Jordan at all, to give us into the hands of the Amorites, to destroy us? Would that we had been content to dwell beyond the Jordan! **8** O Lord, what can I say, when Israel has turned their backs before their enemies? **9** For the Canaanites and all the inhabitants of the land will hear of it and will surround us and cut off our name from the earth. And what will you do for your great name?'"

At first, this seems like a reasonable response from Joshua—pleading with God in a time of distress. However, what came next in the scripture profoundly changed the way I view prayer:

10 "The Lord said to Joshua, 'Get up! Why have you fallen on your face? **11** Israel has sinned; they have transgressed my covenant that I commanded them; they have taken some of the devoted things; they have stolen and lied and put them among their own belongings. **12** Therefore, the people of Israel cannot stand before their enemies. They turn their backs before their enemies, because they have become devoted for destruction. I will be with you no more, unless you destroy the devoted things from among you.'"

Wow. Not the response I would have expected from God. But when God is passionate about something, He often repeats it:

13 "'Get up! Consecrate the people and say, "Consecrate yourselves for tomorrow; for thus says the Lord, God of Israel, 'There are devoted things in your midst, O Israel. You cannot stand before your enemies until you take away the devoted things from among you.'"

Reflection

There are times in life when our posture before God is not what it should be. Yes, there are moments when we need to stop, fall to our knees, and pray. However, there are also times when God has already given us clear instructions, and we have simply failed to comply. Are we approaching God, asking Him to fix things when He has already given us the direction we need to follow?

Things to Consider:

- What are you unwilling to let go of?
- Are you trying to bring people or things along on a journey that God has called only you to at this time?
- Are you discerning what went wrong and why, or are you blaming God for not receiving the outcome you expected?

Making the Prayer Personal:

"Lord, I have sought Your guidance about _____, _____, _____—things in which You have already given me direction and instruction. Today, I ask for the strength to surrender _____, _____, _____, which I have refused to part with. Father in Heaven, please forgive me for any disobedience, whether known or unknown. Help me remember Your direction and not blame You or others for my own failure to do what You have asked of me. Thank You, Lord, for being a God I can always come to. And thank You for being a God who not only sees and hears but also guides and instructs."

Scripture:

Psalm 32:8

"I will instruct you and teach you in the way you should go; I will counsel you with my eye upon you."

Proverbs 28:13

"Whoever conceals their sins does not prosper, but the one who confesses and renounces them finds mercy."

CHAPTER 3

LOOKING BEYOND

As seen in the book of Joshua, God often makes things very clear for us. Yet, it may be the very thing we refuse to confront that hinders us from receiving what we seek—even in prayer. In my own life, there have been times when I've heard from God, whether through a sermon, in prayer, or even during everyday conversations. We need to let go of the notion that God only speaks to us in one way or through specific people we want to hear from. God can use any method He chooses. The real question is, are you willing to receive it?

Imagine your prayer is for transportation to get to a new job. What if God provides transportation, but it's a rusty old car with no heat or air conditioning, even though it runs like a champ? Would you be willing to drive that car, or would you be more concerned about what your family, friends, or coworkers might say? So often, we miss out on blessings and answered prayers because they aren't packaged the way we expect. This doesn't just apply to material things—it's true for relationships as well.

Picture someone who has gone through several unfulfilling relationships, whether abusive or not. Their prayer might be, "Lord, send me someone who will love me, uplift me, and be faithful, kind, and caring." Then, God places someone in their life, but they only focus on the surface—what the person has or how they look—without paying attention to the very qualities they had prayed for. When they overlook the person God sent and seek other opportunities, they're left disappointed when those relationships fail. And then, they direct their frustration at God.

I'm not suggesting you should lower your standards or not have any. But I am asking, have you considered that God may have already answered your prayer, and you just weren't paying attention?

Reflection

Have there been things you prayed for that God provided, but you were too blinded to see? Are there areas in your life where you've missed the opportunity to recognize God's answered prayers?

Things to Consider:

- What have you asked from God that you've ignored because it wasn't what you expected, or didn't come from the person you anticipated?
- Have you been too focused on outward appearances or concerned with the aesthetics?

Making the Prayer Personal

Dear Lord, I humbly come to you today, asking for Your help in identifying areas where I've missed opportunities—where I prayed, yet overlooked the answers You provided. Lord, please guide me in the areas of _____, _____, and _____, where I've focused more on appearance than on what I truly sought from you in prayer. Help me to discern what you have specifically for me. Father, I thank you in advance for your love and for being present, even when I fail to recognize it.

Scripture

Colossians 3:23

"Whatever you do, work heartily, as for the Lord and not for men."

CHAPTER 4

HIS WILL, HIS TIMING

Now, let's switch things up. Maybe for you, it wasn't a relationship or a car—it could have been a position or a new job. Let's say you're highly gifted and talented at what you do. You believe it's a blessing for any company to have you on their team. However, after a few years, you start feeling that you should be recognized or compensated more for the value you bring. You pray about it as you apply for a new job or position, but you don't get it. How does that make you feel? Do you become angry with leadership? Do you grow resentful? Do you turn into someone others no longer recognize?

Sometimes, God moves us into new places or removes us from where we are. The question is, are you willing to make that shift? Or are you resistant to change, stuck in the comfort of where you are?

Perhaps God has delayed or even denied that position you prayed for, not because you aren't talented enough, but because there are emotional or interpersonal challenges you need to address first. I've seen people step into roles only to damage their reputation because they weren't emotionally prepared. This doesn't just apply to professional settings—it's true in intimate relationships, family dynamics, and decision-making in general. Sometimes, God's "no" is actually a blessing.

Reflection

Have there been things you prayed for where God said no? How do you respond when your prayers aren't answered the way you expected?

Things to Consider:

- Is what you're praying for aligned with God's will, or is it simply something you want?
- Are there good reasons you feel God may have said no?
- What are your true motivations behind the prayer?

Making the Prayer Personal

Dear Lord, I acknowledge that my ways are not your ways. Sometimes, I struggle with accepting what you want for me versus what I desire for myself. Your Word says that you will direct our path, and today, I ask for Your help in managing my emotions when my prayers are delayed or denied. Help me understand whether my motivations were right or wrong. Lord, show me how to address my known faults: _____, _____, and _____, as well as the hidden ones I have yet to confront.

Scripture

Jeremiah 33:3

"Call to me and I will answer you, and will tell you great and hidden things that you have not known."

CHAPTER 5

OUT OF YOUR COMFORT ZONE

God saying "no" isn't always the case. Sometimes, though, we find ourselves feeling angry or discontent when He interrupts our comfortable lives. If you've ever lost a job, been reassigned, or faced a significant shift—like retirement, a breakup, or the end of a friendship—you know how difficult these transitions can be. I've experienced it too. I was in a comfortable position, and everything seemed to be going well—until I was suddenly let go. I remember being upset with God, wondering what I had done to deserve such a major life challenge. In my case, I had moved halfway across the country to pursue what I believed God had called me to do. The challenge wasn't that I hadn't fulfilled my calling—I had. But what I didn't realize at the time was that God's plan for me was temporary, while I had made it permanent.

I'm sure you've also held on to relationships, jobs, or situations longer than you should have. Maybe you were the one who stayed in a relationship or position when it was time to move on. Let's say you're an excellent nurse, educator, supervisor, lawyer, police officer, logistics worker, social worker, therapist, or partner. Then, out of nowhere, the job, relationship, or friendship ends. In the middle of it all, you might be praying, as I did, for God to maintain your comfort where you are. But what if God's disruption of your comfort was intentional? What if it was His way of nudging you in a different direction, to push you higher, beyond what you were used to, so that you could grow stronger, wiser, and better? In that case, our prayers for comfort come into direct conflict with God's plan for growth in our lives.

Let's also think about complacency. Have you ever seen someone stay in a position too long, only to become less effective over time? Sometimes, we—yes, even you and me—can become complacent in our calling, abilities, leadership, and relationships. We see this with King David toward the end of his reign. He was no longer as effective as he had once been and failed to address important issues, which led to confusion and unrest. Sometimes, our inability to address the challenges before us can have negative consequences not only for ourselves but also for those we lead or those in relationship with us.

God's disruptions, though uncomfortable, are often His way of getting our attention. We may not realize it at first, but He's moving us to a place of growth, renewal, and purpose. When we're too focused on staying comfortable, we might miss out on the greater things He has in store for us. It's in these moments of discomfort and transition that God is often preparing us for something better. The key is to trust His timing, even when it feels like we're losing something we're not ready to let go of. When we finally surrender, we discover that God's plans are always far better than our own.

Reflection

Are there areas in your life where you're upset or perhaps indifferent when your comfort is challenged? How does this impact your prayer life? Do you find yourself praying more, or withdrawing? Is your current assignment in life coming to an end? We often cling to things that hold meaning for us, whether material items, relationships, careers, businesses, or status.

Things to Consider:

- Are the things you're praying for in alignment with God's desires for your life, or are they in contrast?
- How well do you handle change?
- What specifically about change makes you uncomfortable?

Making the Prayer Personal

Dear Lord, I admit that change can be difficult for me, especially depending on the situation. I know there are things I've asked for_____, _____, _____that may not have been in your will for my life, either for now or ever. Please help me embrace change in a way that is pleasing to you. Lord, help me see opportunities in what lies ahead, rather than focusing on what I've lost or what's new and unfamiliar. Help me with my attitude and emotions, and give me the strength to count my blessings and seek you, even in times of discomfort.

Scripture

Jeremiah 29:11
"For I know the plans I have for you, declares the Lord, plans for welfare and not for evil, to give you a future and a hope."

CHAPTER 6

BELIEVING

Often in prayer, you may speak words that are near and dear to your heart. Depending on where you are in your faith journey, you might find yourself simply going through the motions, not truly expecting anything to happen, but secretly hoping it will. Trust me, you're not alone. Even as a pastor, I wrestle with faith through prayer. I've heard it all—comments like, "I don't like praying because I don't want to be disappointed," or, "I'm skeptical about prayer; what if God rejects my request?" If this resonates with you, know that you are not alone. Even Jesus' disciples struggled with faith.

Let's take a look at Matthew 10:1:

"And He called His twelve disciples to Him and gave them authority over unclean spirits, to cast them out, and to heal every disease and affliction."

However, just a few chapters later, the disciples were tested. In Matthew 17, we read:

14 And when they had come to the multitude, a man came to Him, kneeling down to Him and saying, 15 "Lord, have mercy on my son, for he is an epileptic and suffers severely; for he often falls into the fire and often into the water. 16 So I brought him to your disciples, but they could not cure him." 17 Then Jesus answered and said, "O faithless and perverse generation, how long shall I be with you? How long shall I bear with you? Bring him here to me." 18 And Jesus rebuked the demon, and it came out of him; and the child was cured from that very hour. 19 Then the disciples came to Jesus privately and said, "Why could we not cast it out?" 20 So Jesus said to them, "Because of your unbelief; for assuredly, I say to you, if you have faith as a mustard seed, you will say to this mountain, 'Move from here to there,' and it will move; and nothing will be impossible for you." (NKJV)

Wow, right? Even Jesus' own disciples, who had been given power and authority, doubted—not only in Christ but in themselves. As believers, we too experience doubt and uncertainty at times. Joshua, in the Old Testament, is another example. In Joshua 7, we see that his posture wasn't right—he was on his face, praying to God about why they were not victorious in battle, even though instruction had already been given to him.

Similarly, in the New Testament, we see the disciples asking Jesus why they couldn't cast out the demon from the young boy. Faith played a huge role in their struggle, but Jesus also points out something else in verse 21:

"However, this kind does not go out except by prayer and fasting."

When we think about our prayer life, it's easy to get caught up in the hustle and bustle of everyday demands. If you have a family, you're probably juggling multiple responsibilities. If you're single, you might be balancing just as much between school, work, and extra-curricular activities. For those who attend church, add in the potential roles and responsibilities that come with that. Yes, even church can feel like busy work if you're so caught up in "doing" that you fail to truly be present. Attendance doesn't necessarily equal relationship. As my daughter says, life can just be "life-ing"—meaning it's extra busy.

When the disciples approached the multitudes, they probably had no idea what to expect. And they might have thought, "Hey, we've got Jesus with us—if anything difficult happens, He'll handle it."

Reflection

Has God given you the power and authority to do things that you lack the faith to accomplish? Could it be that you haven't devoted the time and effort necessary to prepare for the areas where prayer is most needed?

To put it another way: Have your prayers become ineffective because you haven't properly prepared yourself as you enter new stages or challenges in life?

Things to Consider:

- Identify areas in your faith that are lacking.
- What struggles, if any, do you have in trusting God with the power He's given you?
- Have you become so busy that you've neglected to focus on what your prayer life should be?

Making the Prayer Personal

Dear God, at times, I struggle with my faith. I've been ashamed to admit this, but I know you look past the outer appearance and see my heart. Lord, I continually struggle with _____, _____, _____. Help me in my faith journey to see you more clearly. Renew a fire within me so I may feel close to you again.

Lord, you've given me power over _____, _____ and gifted me with _____, _____, but I haven't used these to their full potential. Quiet my spirit so I can engage with you in a meaningful way. Don't let me become so preoccupied with life and doing things that I lose sight of your call and direction.

Scripture

James 1:5-6
"If any of you lacks wisdom, let him ask of God, who gives to all liberally and without reproach, and it will be given to him."

Philippians 4:19
And my God shall supply all your need according to His riches in glory by Christ Jesus.

CHAPTER 7

DEATH, DYING, HEALING

Conflicting Thoughts

One of the most challenging times in life is when we are praying for a family member who is suffering from illness. As family members, we naturally want as much time with our loved ones as possible. This is perfectly understandable. Early in my chaplaincy career, I encountered a situation that I still consider one of the most difficult. I had the privilege of spending time with a middle-aged patient in the hospital who expressed to me that he had lived a good life and was ready to go on to be with the Lord. At the same time, however, his spouse was praying fervently for him to stay alive, asking that everything possible be done to keep him with her.

Here was the dilemma: the patient, praying for peace and release, was ready to leave this world, while his wife, in deep distress, was praying for a miracle to keep him alive. As the chaplain, I found myself caught between these two conflicting prayers. Should I align myself with the husband, who was my patient? Or should I stand with his wife, who was desperate and heartbroken? This conflict was all too familiar to me, as I had experienced the pain of losing multiple family members who were very close to me.

If you were the spouse in this situation, it would be entirely natural to feel anger—not only toward your loved one but perhaps even toward God. For some, the loss of a loved one may feel like the final blow to their faith. When we pray for healing, and the outcome is not what we hoped for, our faith can be shaken. In this particular case, the husband passed away that very night. As I reflected on it, I found myself wrestling with a difficult question: Whose prayer did God answer? Did He answer the husband's prayer by granting him peace and easing his suffering? Or was the wife's prayer unheard or meaningless?

These are the kinds of questions that can challenge the very foundation of our faith. In this case, both the husband and wife were believers. They deeply loved one another. The husband never blamed God for his illness. In fact, he was profoundly grateful to God for the life he had lived, for his marriage to his high school sweetheart, and for the children and grandchildren they had shared. His wife, though heartbroken, was eventually able to find solace in reflecting on the blessings they had received over the past 30 years.

When we face death, illness, or the loss of a loved one, it is entirely natural to feel anger, isolation, or confusion. These emotions are part of the grieving process. It's important to acknowledge and honor how you feel. But know this: if you prayed and did not receive the outcome you hoped for, it does not mean that your prayer wasn't heard or that you did something wrong. Sometimes, the answers to our prayers are not what we expect, but they are still part of a divine plan that we may not fully understand in the moment.

Let's consider the Apostle Paul as an example. Paul was responsible for writing two-thirds of the New Testament. Throughout the biblical narratives, he is seen performing miracles and healing people he encountered. Yet, in 2 Corinthians 12, Paul himself struggles with what he refers to as a "thorn in the flesh":

"And lest I should be exalted above measure by the abundance of the revelations, a thorn in the flesh was given to me, a messenger of Satan to buffet me, lest I be exalted above measure. Concerning this thing I pleaded with the Lord three times that it might depart from me. And He said to me, 'My grace is sufficient for you, for My strength is made perfect in weakness.' Therefore, most gladly I will rather boast in my infirmities, that the power of Christ may rest upon me. Therefore I take pleasure in infirmities, in reproaches, in needs, in persecutions, in distresses, for Christ's sake. For when I am weak, then I am strong." (2 Corinthians 12:7-10)

Now, imagine how frustrating this must have been for Paul. He could perform miracles, lay hands on the sick, and they would recover—yet he couldn't heal himself. This passage may not provide immediate comfort, but it serves to remind us that sometimes, despite our most heartfelt prayers, certain things are left in God's hands and according to His will.

In life, we won't always get answers to all our "whys." However, we must find a way to trust God, even when our prayers go unanswered.

Reflection

Have you ever prayed for someone's health to improve, only to find it didn't? Have you considered that the person you were praying for might have desired something entirely different than you? What emotions did you experience? What exactly were you angry about? Take this time to dig deeper.

Have you blamed yourself for their ailment or death? Have you directed that anger toward others? How has their passing affected you and your faith?

Things to Consider:

- It is not your fault.
- Have you been honest with yourself and God about your emotions and feelings?
- Have you sought resources, such as grief counseling?

Making the Prayer Personal

Dear Lord,

I am wrestling with anger and grief. I truly love you, but the ailment and/or loss of my loved one has brought me anguish that words cannot express. I constantly feel _____, _____, _____, which I cannot escape on my own. Lord, help me through this pain so that I may once again be in a right relationship with you. Give me the strength to use the necessary resources to walk through my journey of healing and forgiveness. I understand that I don't have to do this alone; even if no one is physically present to help me, you are always close. Help me to feel your presence. Be by my side and strengthen me during this time.

Scripture

1 Peter 5:6-7
"Therefore humble yourselves under the mighty hand of God, that He may exalt you in due time, casting all your care upon Him, for He cares for you."

Psalm 34:18
"The Lord is near to the brokenhearted and saves the crushed in spirit." (ESV)

CHAPTER 8

RELATIONSHIPS IN MARRIAGE

Prayer in relationships and marriages can be incredibly complex. I've witnessed God perform miracles in some of the most broken relationships, while I've also seen what appeared to be thriving marriages dissolve unexpectedly. While prayer can certainly support the health of relationships, it is not always a standalone solution.

Have you ever been in a relationship where you sought God to sort things out? As a minister and a former mental health professional, I have had the privilege of journeying alongside couples navigating their relationships. In counseling sessions, I often sit back and ask general questions like, "What brings you here?" Some couples jump right to the point, expressing their frustrations: "I don't like this," or "I don't like that." They share feelings of neglect, lack of communication, and the absence of physical affection, or they confess that they've fallen out of love. In some cases, couples are remarkably transparent, admitting that they married for practical reasons—perhaps because of the children, societal expectations, or simply because they felt there was "nothing better to do" after being together for so long.

In my professional opinion, some people enter marriage to fill a void, and this phenomenon is not limited to those who are people of faith or active in the church. They are not exempt from these patterns. I believe in love, and I know many happily married couples exist, but let's take a deeper look at the who, what, when, and why of marriage.

More often than not, I've observed that people in unhappy or broken marriages were not adequately prepared before entering into their commitments. While there are certainly exceptions such as cases of domestic abuse, whether verbal, emotional, or physical many struggles arise from unmet expectations and a lack of understanding about the realities of marriage. Life can throw unexpected challenges at us: illnesses, the loss of a child or employment, or even a partner's loss of motivation.

Over the years, I've seen more faith-based institutions recommending outside counseling for couples. However, not all churches or places of worship have done an effective job in preparing individuals for marriage. It's essential to have realistic expectations, set achievable goals, and understand the true commitment involved in navigating the ups and downs of marriage or committed relationships.

In my experience within church settings, premarital counseling is often conducted by a minister and their spouse or an older couple who have been married for many years. Typically, they cover the biblical responsibilities of each partner, referencing notable scriptures such as Ephesians 5 and 6. They may discuss some key reasons marriages end in divorce, such as finances and intimacy. However, I strongly suggest that every couple in a committed relationship contemplating marriage also seek the guidance of a professional relationship or marriage counselor. This can be an important complement to any church counseling or spiritual guidance they receive. Not all counseling is created equal; it's crucial to find a therapist who will engage with both partners and challenge them to grow.

During my time in seminary, I took a course on pastoral care and spiritual disciplines. My professor shared an experience counseling a couple in the church who wanted to get married. Both individuals were deeply committed to God and loved each other. While my professor, a trained counselor, knew them well and recognized their individual strengths, he also understood that they had significant differences.

As they proceeded with marriage counseling, my professor worked to stretch their understanding of what marriage truly entails. They had a solid grasp of the biblical principles, having grown up in the church with a strong foundational understanding. However, when it came to their individual desires for life and relationships, they began to second-guess their decision to marry. Ultimately, they chose not to continue with the marriage process, realizing that despite their deep friendship and shared faith, they were not well-suited for a lifelong partnership. Instead, they decided to remain friends.

But why? Isn't love enough? With God, all things are possible, right? All it takes is faith the size of a mustard seed. Interestingly, both individuals later married different partners and went on to have happy marriages. The moral of this story is that while having commonalities—including faith—can be important, it doesn't necessarily guarantee a match made in heaven. Marriage involves much deeper compatibility.

Divorce and Prayer

When divorce becomes reality, prayer is a very good avenue to work through the storm that sometimes accompanies such a choice. A couple may pray for guidance through painful separation so as to find their way around daunting circumstances. Prayer may comfort and remind one of self-worth to help heal the hurt of a broken relationship.

Praying can also lead to reconciliation as the couples reflect on their decision and how they can forgive each other. Sometimes, praying for an ex-spouse can be done by asking for peace and healing from both individuals involved. Therefore, through prayers, one can obtain closure and a way forward to continue rebuilding or living a new chapter of life.

While faith and love are the basic building blocks for any relationship, let alone marriage, compatibility of the couple and a shared vision also play an important role. Couples should not feel hesitant in seeking spiritual and professional guidance to establish a healthy and long-lasting relationship.

Reflection

When you are praying for your relationship are you only praying for the other person to change? Should your prayer include how you respond or don't respond to the other person.

Things to Consider:

- **Personal Prayer Reflection:** Are your prayers focused only on changing the other person, or do they include requests for God to help you respond with patience, compassion, and understanding?
- **Realistic Expectations:** Do you hold any expectations that may be causing strain in your relationship? Reflect on whether these expectations are realistic and discuss them with your partner.
- **Seek Guidance:** Consider speaking with a professional counselor or trusted spiritual advisor to help navigate any challenges. Both spiritual and professional support can be incredibly beneficial.

Making the Prayer Personal

"Lord, I bring my relationship before You, acknowledging that I cannot change anyone but myself. Help me to approach my partner with an open heart and a willingness to listen and understand. Show me how to be patient and compassionate in my words and actions. If there is any part of me that needs healing, reveal it to me, and guide me in Your love. Teach us, as a couple, to seek You together in unity. Help us to strengthen our bond, and if reconciliation is needed, give us the humility to forgive. Guide us toward a relationship built on faith, trust, and shared purpose. Amen."

CHAPTER 9

THE IMPORTANCE OF PREPARATION IN PRAYER

Many times, prayer is considered that direct hotline to God where we present our hopes, desires, and wishes. And always in prayers, we ask for things we are desperate for, like getting a good grade in some test. But what is important to be underlined here is that prayer is not some sort of magic lamp out of which our every wish should spring into being without an effort from us. After all, as the age-old aphorism goes, "God helps those who help themselves." This precept is indeed true, be it regarding our academic lives or otherwise.

In Proverbs 21:5

"The plans of the diligent lead to profit as surely as haste leads to poverty." (NIV)

This verse underscores the importance of diligence and preparation in our lives. When we are diligent in our studies, we are honoring the responsibilities entrusted to us. The same principle applies to our spiritual lives: God calls us to be faithful stewards of our time and abilities. While praying for guidance and understanding is essential, it is equally important to take action by studying and preparing thoroughly.

Prayer is not just about asking God for favors; it's about building a relationship with Him and aligning our actions with our intentions. When we pray for a good grade, we must reflect on our commitment to studying and preparing adequately. James 2:17 reminds us:

"Thus also faith by itself, if it does not have works, is dead." (NKJV)

This verse serves as a reminder that our faith must be demonstrated through our actions. If we pray for success without putting in the necessary work, we are not fully engaging in the partnership God desires with us. It's like trying to plant seeds without preparing the soil; we cannot expect to see a fruitful harvest without doing the work required.

As Christians, we have a responsibility to honor God through our actions. This includes how we approach our education. When we prepare for a test, we are not just studying for ourselves; we are serving God with our efforts. Colossians 3:23-24 encourages us:

"Whatever you do, work heartily, as for the Lord and not for men, knowing that from the Lord you will receive the inheritance as your reward. You are serving the Lord Christ." (ESV)

This scripture reminds us that our studies and efforts should be an act of worship. When we study diligently and pray earnestly, we invite God into our academic journey.

Reflection

When we pray for a good grade, it's essential to assess our commitment to preparation. Did we set aside time to study? Did we seek help when needed? Are we genuinely giving our best effort? These are vital questions to consider as we align our prayers with our actions.

Things to Consider:

- Are there areas in your life where you find yourself relying solely on prayer without taking necessary steps to prepare?
- How can you cultivate a more balanced approach to prayer and preparation in your academic life?
- What practical steps can you take to ensure you are adequately prepared for upcoming challenges?

Making the Prayer Personal

Dear Heavenly Father, I come to you today with a humble heart. I know that I cannot expect to receive a good grade on my _____ if I haven't put in the effort to_____. Help me to be diligent and responsible in my preparation. I pray for wisdom and understanding as I work through my studies.

Lord, I ask that You bless my efforts and guide my thoughts as I prepare. Help me to remember that my work is ultimately for You and not just for grades. May I find strength in Your presence as I balance my studies with my relationship with You. Thank You for Your grace and support in my academic journey. Amen.

Proverbs 16:3:

"Commit to the Lord whatever you do, and He will establish your plans." (NIV)

Matthew 7:7:

"Ask, and it will be given to you; seek, and you will find; knock, and it will be opened to you." (NKJV)

CHAPTER 10

PRAYING THROUGH ANGER AND DISAPPOINTMENT

In our walk with God, feelings of anger and disappointment can sometimes seem like barriers in our faith journey. Life's uncertainties may lead us to experience a mix of stress, anxiety, and even depression, threatening to cloud our emotions and shake the foundation of our trust in God. Yet, learning to bring these emotions to God in prayer, rather than letting them control us, is a powerful act of trust and surrender. Faith, after all, is not merely about the joyful moments; it's about standing firm in our connection with God, even when the path forward feels difficult.

In the Bible, we see countless examples of people grappling with similar feelings of impatience and disappointment. One such powerful story is of the Israelites in the wilderness. They had been freed from bondage in Egypt, yet the journey through the wilderness wasn't the immediate promise of abundance that they anticipated. The wilderness was not a pleasant, straightforward path; it was filled with trials and tests. God didn't abandon them but instead used the wilderness as a place of transformation. The Israelites had to confront their bad habits, remnants of their time in Egypt, and learn to put their faith and trust wholly in God.

This wilderness season was necessary for three main reasons: First, it was an opportunity for God to remind the Israelites of who He was—a faithful provider who delivered them from slavery. Second, it was a chance to uproot negative patterns that were formed in bondage. And finally, it was an opportunity for their hearts to fully turn toward Him, learning to rely on His guidance rather than their own limited understanding.

The Israelites' impatience and frustration mirrored feelings we often have today. They questioned, doubted, and tried to take matters into their own hands, fearing that God's timing wasn't aligning with their needs. How many of us have done the same in our own lives? We begin to anticipate potential problems, worry about what might happen, and, instead of being still and waiting on God, we start making our own moves. This tendency to jump into action before seeking God's guidance or trusting in His timing often stems from anxiety and a desire to control the situation.

In my personal journey, I've experienced moments when I've sabotaged my own prayers by letting anxiety and frustration take over. In those moments, I tried to 'fix' things, moving ahead of God, thinking that He wasn't acting fast enough. In hindsight, those decisions didn't bring me the peace or resolution I was seeking. Instead, they led to ripple effects and further challenges, creating more problems that I eventually had to bring back to God in prayer.

Trusting God requires us to let go, especially when we don't understand what He's doing or why He's silent. Our emotions are real and valid, but they shouldn't become the drivers of our faith. God wants us to bring our burdens, fears, and disappointments to Him in prayer. When we hold back, we block ourselves from experiencing the peace that only He can provide.

Learning to trust and be still in prayer is a powerful antidote to the anticipatory worry that so often drives us. God isn't asking us to ignore our anger, disappointment, or frustration; He's inviting us to surrender it to Him. By doing so, we release the hold these emotions have on us and open ourselves to His healing and guidance.

Reflection Questions:

- What are the emotions that tend to drive your decisions? Are there times you've let impatience or worry take the lead instead of trusting in God?
- How do you feel when you think about surrendering your frustrations and anxieties to God in prayer? What might be holding you back?

- What lessons can you draw from the story of the Israelites in the wilderness, and how can you apply them to your own faith journey?

Things to Consider:

- Reflect on a time when taking action before seeking God's guidance led to unforeseen challenges. What would you have done differently?
- Consider the patterns and habits that may be lingering from past experiences. What steps can you take to address them and draw closer to God?
- Think about your own "wilderness" experiences. How can you reframe these moments as opportunities for growth and trust in God?

Making the Prayer Personal:

"Lord, I bring to You my frustrations, my disappointments, and my impatience. I confess that there are times when I've moved ahead of You, trying to solve things on my own because I doubted Your timing. Help me, God, to release control and trust in Your perfect plan. Teach me to be still and allow Your peace to fill my heart, no matter the situation. Remind me, as You did with the Israelites, that You are faithful and that You work all things for my good. Strengthen my faith and help me to wait with patience, knowing that You are with me every step of the way. Amen."

CHAPTER 11

FINAL WORDS

Are you praying about the issue itself or just its effects? Let me explain. Imagine you're praying to God to heal your heart after a breakup, yet you continue to date the same type of person who contributed to your pain. Shouldn't your prayer focus more on asking the Lord to help you combat the desires of your flesh, especially since you tend to be vulnerable around certain individuals?

Consider another example: you might be praying for deliverance from drinking, drugs, gambling, smoking, or even excessive social media use. But are any of these addictions the root of the issue, or are they merely coping mechanisms you use to escape deeper problems? While prayer is undeniably powerful, it should be directed at the root of an issue rather than just its symptoms. This distinction can be confusing for believers. Even the Bible acknowledges our struggles in knowing how to pray, as stated in Romans 8:26:

"Likewise, the Spirit also helps in our weaknesses. For we do not know what we should pray for as we ought, but the Spirit Himself makes intercession for us with groaning which cannot be uttered."

The Bible is rich with examples of devout men and women who have poured out their hearts in prayer. The Psalms, for instance, are filled with prayers from David expressing anguish, pain, fear, depression, and loneliness. It's essential to recognize that God may not answer every prayer in the way we hope, as some requests might not align with His perfect will. Some challenges we face could be tests of our faith or consequences of our own actions or inactions.

Regardless of the circumstances, the most important thing is to continue building your relationship with God. When things don't go your way, that's the time to draw closer to Him, not further away. God desires your whole heart. He is big enough to handle your anger, your doubts, and even your temper tantrums. When you engage with God, make it a point to express gratitude, not just to ask for things.

Too often, we place all the responsibility on God to make things right. As I've mentioned earlier, sometimes God has given us the power and authority to resolve our issues ourselves. Yet, it can be fear or unwillingness that holds us back. In these moments, seek God more earnestly than ever. Create a sacred space in your home, car, or even in nature where you can connect with Him without distractions—a place where you can be truly transparent.

Also, consider that God sometimes desires us to actively participate in the prayers we lift up. Ask yourself: is there any responsibility on your part in the prayer you are offering? Are you genuinely willing to do your part? Remember, prayer is not just about seeking help; it's also about partnering with God in the journey toward healing and growth.

There are things we often fail to prepare for, yet we seek God's intervention on our behalf. But are we asking God for divine intervention in situations He never intended for us to be a part of?

I firmly believe that God can do anything. He has the power to show up, show out, and move mountains. But are we asking God for something out of genuine need or mere want? While wanting isn't inherently bad, we must consider whether what we desire will deepen our faith or become a distraction.

When God is silent, are we disciplined enough to remain still? Can we exercise patience? Have you forgotten the instructions? When God moves, He often provides some form of guidance. Are you surrounding yourself with wise counsel? I've found myself in precarious situations due to the voices I chose to listen to.

Do you have the right posture? It can be frustrating to discern when it's time to kneel in prayer and when it's time to take action.

Are you willing to try again? Sometimes, after experiencing failure or not achieving the desired outcome, we can feel discouraged.

But take heart—God truly cares for you. Remember that He is always with you, guiding your steps and inviting you to deepen your relationship with Him. Stay encouraged as you navigate your journey of faith, knowing that every prayer, every effort, and every moment spent with Him contributes to your growth.

Final Prayer

Heavenly Father, we thank You for Your unwavering love and support in our lives. Help us to seek You wholeheartedly, directing our prayers toward the root of our struggles. Grant us the strength to confront our challenges and the wisdom to recognize our responsibilities in our prayers. May we find comfort in Your presence and continue to grow in our relationship with You. Encourage us to remain faithful and patient, trusting in Your perfect timing. In Jesus' name, we pray, Amen.

www.ingramcontent.com/pod-product-compliance
Lightning Source LLC
Chambersburg PA
CBHW070551090426
42735CB00013B/3153